D1156653

CATS SET I

ABYSSINIAN CATS

Tamara L. Britton
ABDO Publishing Company

visit us at
www.abdopublishing.com

Published by ABDO Publishing Company, 8000 West 78th Street, Edina, Minnesota 55439. Copyright © 2011 by Abdo Consulting Group, Inc. International copyrights reserved in all countries. No part of this book may be reproduced in any form without written permission from the publisher. The Checkerboard Library™ is a trademark and logo of ABDO Publishing Company.

Printed in the United States of America, North Mankato, Minnesota.
042010
092010

 PRINTED ON RECYCLED PAPER

Cover Photo: Photo by Helmi Flick
Interior Photos: Alamy pp. 17, 19; AP Images p. 15;
    Photo by Helmi Flick pp. 5, 9, 11, 13, 21; Peter Arnold pp. 6–7

Editor: Megan M. Gunderson
Art Direction & Cover Design: Neil Klinepier

Library of Congress Cataloging-in-Publication Data

Britton, Tamara L., 1963-
  Abyssinian cats / Tamara L. Britton.
      p. cm. -- (Cats)
  Includes index.
  ISBN 978-1-61613-397-9
  1. Abyssinian cat--Juvenile literature. I. Title.
  SF449.A28B75 2011
  636.8'26--dc22
                                    2010013412

CONTENTS

LIONS, TIGERS, AND CATS

More than 3,500 years ago, people in Egypt began taming wildcats. These cats hunted rats and mice that invaded buildings where grain was stored. The Egyptians believed cats brought prosperity and good fortune.

Domestic cats can trace their ancestry back to these African wildcats. Today, there are more than 40 different **breeds** of domestic cats.

These cats all belong to the family **Felidae**, which contains 37 different species. Lions, tigers, leopards, cheetahs, and pumas are also members of this family.

Big cat species share similar qualities with **domestic** cats. All cats use their sharp teeth and claws for hunting. The big cats communicate by roaring. Domestic cats roar, too. But their smaller size shrinks the sound to a meow!

The Abyssinian cat

ABYSSINIAN CATS

The Abyssinian is one of the oldest cat **breeds**. Early Abyssinian lovers did not keep breed records. So, the breed's exact origin is unknown.

Near the end of the 1800s, England was involved in a war in Ethiopia. At the time, Ethiopia was known as Abyssinia. The first Abyssinian cat came to England not long after the fighting ended.

Cat enthusiasts claimed that this first cat was from

Abyssinia. That is how the **breed** got its name. However, scientists later discovered that the Abyssinian cat most likely came from Asia.

The first Abyssinians arrived in North America from England in the early 1900s. Then in 1906, the **Cat Fanciers' Association (CFA)** was founded.

The ruddy-coated Abyssinian has been a recognized breed since the CFA's founding. In 1963, the organization recognized Abyssinians with red coats. It recognized Abyssinians with blue coats in 1984 and those with fawn coats in 1989.

Because of its long, slender legs, the Abyssinian looks like it stands on tiptoe!

QUALITIES

Abyssinians have two speeds, which are on and off! Unless they are eating or sleeping, these busy cats are always on the move. They will play with a toy for hours. But they can be just as amused with a wadded piece of paper.

Abyssinians are athletic and smart. They are curious and good at solving problems. You might find your Abyssinian atop a high perch you thought she could not reach. Then you will know she just applied her intelligence to figure out the way up!

These playful, affectionate cats like being with people. They are good around children as well as other pets.

A toy will bring out your busy Abyssinian's playful nature!

Coat and Color

Abyssinians are known for their distinctive coats. The fur is short, thick, soft, and silky. It is also richly colored.

Much of the coat is **ticked**. Each ticked hair has two or three bands of black, brown, or blue. The cat's undersides, chest, and legs have no ticking.

An Abyssinian's coat color may be ruddy, red, blue, or fawn. Ruddy coats are orange brown with dark brown or black ticking. Red coats are a warm red color with chocolate brown bands. Blue coats are beige with slate blue bands. Fawn coats are pink beige with cocoa brown ticking.

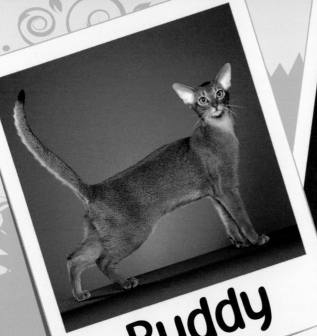

Ruddy

Red

Fawn

Blue

Size

Abyssinians are medium-sized cats with graceful, muscular bodies. Both males and females fall into the same weight range. They can weigh between 6 and 10 pounds (3 and 4.5 kg).

The **breed**'s body shape is long and lean. Slim, fine-boned legs support the cat's slender frame. The Abyssinian's oval-shaped feet are small. Its long tail is thick at the rump. But, it tapers to a slightly rounded tip.

The Abyssinian's head is shaped like a wedge. The cat's large, slightly pointed ears are cupped. Its rounded nose sits between expressive, almond-shaped eyes. These large eyes can be green or gold.

The Abyssinian's cupped ears make it look like it is always listening!

CARE

Cats are naturally clean. They use their rough tongues to bathe their fur. Abyssinians should also be groomed weekly with a brush or a comb. This will remove loose hair and keep them from developing hairballs. During **shedding** season, these cats may need a bath.

One natural instinct cats have is to bury their waste. This means you can train your Abyssinian to use a **litter box**. Keep the box in a quiet place away from the cat's food and water. And be sure to remove waste from the box daily.

Outdoors, cats sharpen their claws on trees. Indoors, your cat will need a scratching post where it can sharpen its claws. This will turn the cat's attention away from furniture and carpeting!

Abyssinians can develop medical problems, such as eye trouble. So, it is important to develop a relationship with a veterinarian. This doctor can provide yearly checkups and **vaccines**. He or she can also **spay** or **neuter** your cat.

By age seven, cats are considered seniors. These older cats should visit the veterinarian every six months.

FEEDING

Cats are carnivores. So, your Abyssinian's food should contain protein from beef, poultry, or fish. A good commercial cat food provides all the **nutrients** your cat needs.

There are three kinds of commercial cat food. They are dry, semimoist, and canned. Choose one based on your cat's age, weight, and health. Follow the feeding instructions on the food label.

If you are concerned about your cat's weight, check with your veterinarian. He or she can recommend a healthy feeding schedule.

Abyssinians need plenty of fresh water. Make sure to have some available at all times. Many cats also enjoy an occasional treat. Pet stores carry many commercial cat treats. It is not a good idea to share your treats with your cat!

**Cats can be picky eaters!
You may have to try several
high-quality foods to find
one your cat likes.**

KITTENS

Abyssinians can reproduce by 7 to 12 months of age. After mating, a female Abyssinian is **pregnant** for about 63 to 65 days. The mother can have about three **litters** each year. On average, she gives birth to four kittens in each litter.

At birth, kittens are blind and deaf. Their senses begin to function when they are two weeks old. The kittens begin to play and explore within their first three weeks. By then, their teeth start coming in.

Each day, the kittens should be gently cuddled. This will create calm, friendly pets. Early handling will also prepare them for regular grooming. When the kittens are 12 to 16 weeks old, they can go home with new families.

An Abyssinian kitten's coat is not ticked at birth.
That coloring comes in as the kitten gets older.

Buying a Kitten

So, you have decided an Abyssinian is right for you. Many other cat lovers have made the same decision! The Abyssinian is the **CFA**'s sixth most popular **breed**.

Abyssinian cats are available from a reputable breeder once they are three to four months old. The kittens will have already received their first **vaccines**. The breeder will show you how to register your kitten with the CFA.

The cost of an Abyssinian kitten depends on its markings and **pedigree**. You may spend hundreds of dollars for a kitten from award-winning parents. It is also possible to adopt an Abyssinian from a shelter or a rescue organization.

During their first year, kittens develop behaviors they will have for life. Begin training right away so your kittens will understand acceptable behavior.

Wherever you find your feline companion, you will have a valued friend. A well cared for Abyssinian will be a loving family member for 10 to 15 years.

GLOSSARY

breed - a group of animals sharing the same ancestors and appearance. A breeder is a person who raises animals. Raising animals is often called breeding them.

Cat Fanciers' Association (CFA) - a group that sets the standards for judging all breeds of cats.

domestic - tame, especially relating to animals.

Felidae (FEHL-uh-dee) - the scientific Latin name for the cat family. Members of this family are called felids. They include domestic cats, lions, tigers, leopards, jaguars, cougars, wildcats, lynx, and cheetahs.

litter - all of the kittens born at one time to a mother cat.

litter box - a box filled with cat litter, which is similar to sand. Cats use litter boxes to bury their waste.

neuter (NOO-tuhr) - to remove a male animal's reproductive organs.

nutrient - a substance found in food and used in the body. It promotes growth, maintenance, and repair.

pedigree - a record of an animal's ancestors.

pregnant - having one or more babies growing within the body.

shed - to cast off hair, feathers, skin, or other coverings or parts by a natural process.

spay - to remove a female animal's reproductive organs.

ticked - having hair banded with two or more colors. Ticked markings are called ticking.

vaccine (vak-SEEN) - a shot given to prevent illness or disease.

WEB SITES

To learn more about Abyssinian cats, visit ABDO Publishing Company on the World Wide Web at **www.abdopublishing.com**. Web sites about Abyssinian cats are featured on our Book Links page. These links are routinely monitored and updated to provide the most current information available.

INDEX